Ladybird Picture Books
Indoor Things
Outdoor Things
Things That Go
Things to Wear
Things to Play With

LADYBIRD BOOKS, INC.
Auburn, Maine 04210 U.S.A.
© LADYBIRD BOOKS LTD MCMLXXXVIII
Loughborough, Leicestershire, England

All rights reserved. No part of this publication may be reproduced, stored in a retrieval system, or transmitted in any form or by any means, electronic, mechanical, photocopying, recording or otherwise, without the prior consent of the copyright owner.

Printed in England

Things to Play With

Illustrated by Meryl Henderson

Ladybird Books

red

train

wagon

jack-in-the-box

drum

orange

crayons

ball

puzzle

bulldozer

yellow

rocking horse

teddy bear

puppet

rubber duck

green

chalkboard

pail and shovel

doll

blocks

roller skates

balloon

whistle

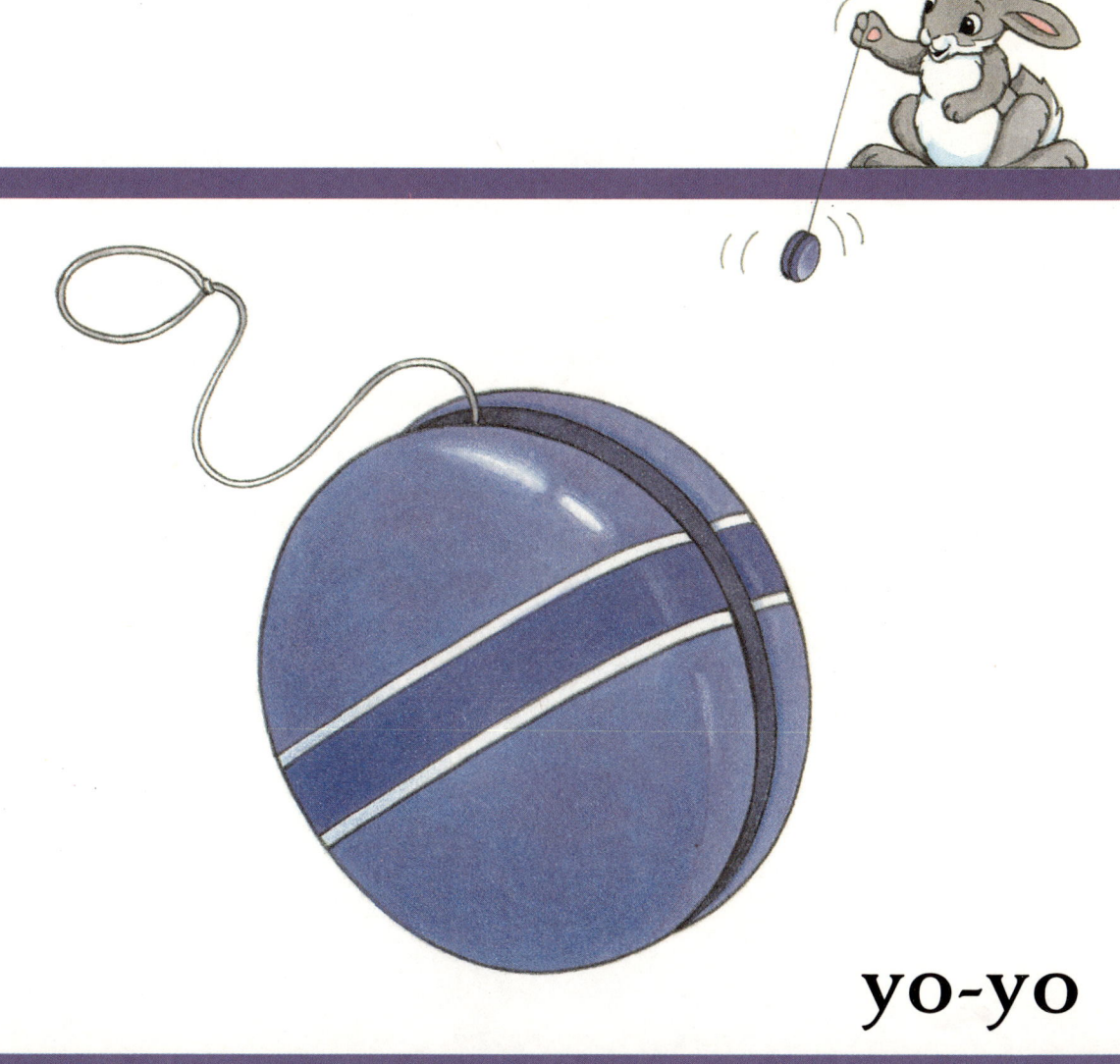

yo-yo

top

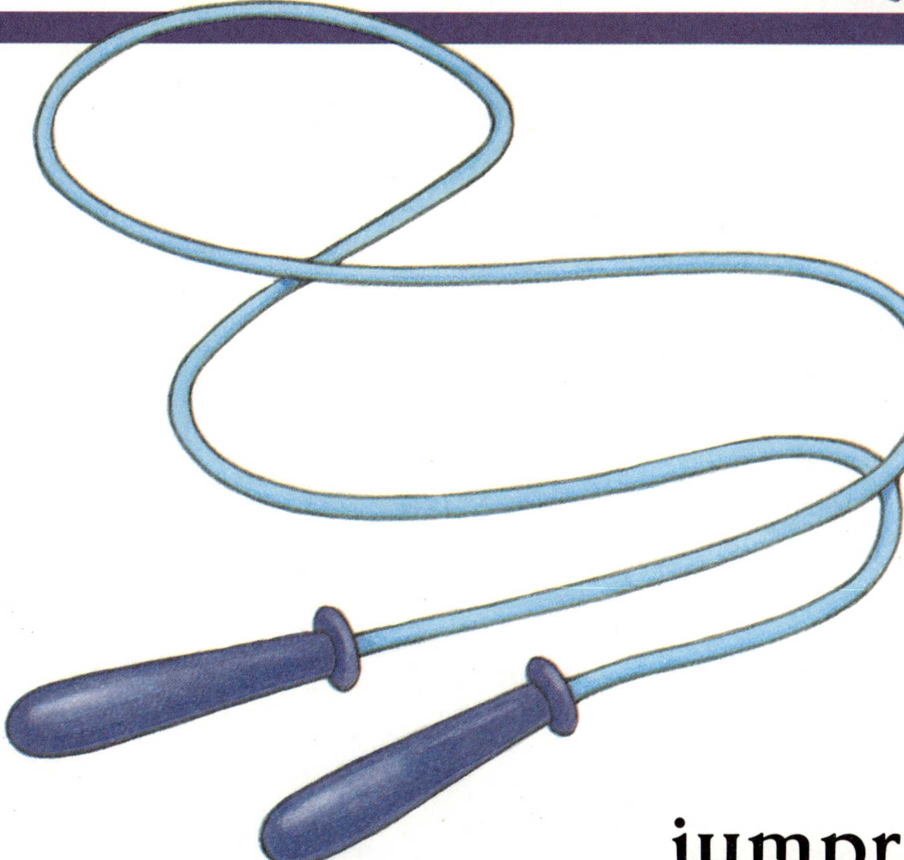

jumprope